D0906300

Michael Faraday

Creative Scientist

by Martin J. Gutnik

 CHILDRENS PRESS®
CHICAGO

PICTURE ACKNOWLEDGMENTS

Historical Pictures Services, Inc., Chicago—Frontispiece, pages 10, 20, 26, 36, 42, 54, 58, 59, 60 (2 photos), 61, 62, 63, 64, 65, 66
Horizon Graphics—illustrations on pages 47, 50, 71, 73, 76
Cover illustration by Len W. Meents

Library of Congress Cataloging in Publication Data

Gutnik, Martin J.
   Michael Faraday, creative scientist.

   Includes index.
   Summary: Examines the life of the English physicist, who rose from a boyhood in the slums of London to make significant discoveries in the study of electricity, magnetism, and light.
   1. Faraday, Michael, 1791-1867—Juvenile literature.
2. Physicists—Great Britain—Biography—Juvenile literature. [1. Faraday, Michael, 1791-1867. 2. Physicists]
I. Title.
QC16.F2G87   1986   530'.092'4 [B] [92]   86-11702
ISBN 0-516-03224-0

 2 3 4 5 6 7 8 9 10 R 95 94 93 92 91 90 89 88 87

Table of Contents

London in the 1860s

Chapter 1

THE EARLY YEARS

It seems as if London, England, has always been a large, sprawling city. Actually, London was once two very small, ancient cities. The Roman city of London was the first village on the banks of the river Thames and was surrounded by a large wall, built at the end of the second century, that was designed for protection against attacks from invaders. A thousand years later, in the same area, the village of Westminster was established by the British royalty. Most of the government offices were located there.

By the beginning of the nineteenth century, London had overgrown the walls of Roman London and had outstretched the borders of Westminster. This was the London that Michael Faraday, who was born on September 27, 1791, would come to know. A terrible worldwide economic depression in 1801 forced James Faraday and his family to move from their run-down house in the London suburb of Newington Butts to an even poorer area on Gilbert Street. The family struggled financially because James, a blacksmith, had rheumatism and so could work only part-time.

Nine-year-old Michael hardly noticed the poverty. As a

youngster, he was extremely curious, and this led him to be a questioner of everything. Michael quizzed his father while they worked together at their blacksmith forge at home. Usually, James listened patiently and tried to answer Michael's questions, but James was a poorly educated man. They both enjoyed their time together, though, and Mr. Faraday was very proud of his smart son.

Michael often worried because he felt that he was different from other people. He asked more questions than anyone else he knew, so was something wrong with him? People seemed to be bothered by his urgent need to know more. The boys and girls who were Michael's age refused to play with him. They did not like his constant probing, and they often made fun of him.

Then there was Michael's teacher who felt bombarded by his questions and in frustration would snap, "Enough, Michael! Now get to your school work and forget all these silly questions." Michael tried to obey his teacher and concentrate on his studies, but he soon became bored and his mind wandered into fantasies. Without realizing it, he would be off on a ship, discovering new worlds, or trekking through some unknown forest, finding new species of plants and animals. His teacher would jolt him back to reality, however, by saying, "Michael, stop your daydreaming!"

Soon Michael felt very lonely. He had no friends, and his

teachers did not understand him. But most disappointing of all was when Michael's father stopped answering his questions. James was frightened, and he often became short-tempered with Michael because he was always thinking about how he could earn money for his family.

Michael wanted to help, but what could he do? Then, thinking about his brother Robert who already had a job, Michael figured that he himself could also get one. "I am thirteen years old now, old enough to hold a job," he said to himself. It was not long before Michael began his job hunt in London.

London in the nineteenth century was a very large city, much as New York or Chicago is today. But the thought of looking for work in London did not frighten Michael. To the contrary, Michael felt challenged and excited by the thought of this new experience.

Michael was not familiar with most parts of the city, and, like most Londoners, he rarely journeyed out of the suburb where he lived. As Michael roamed the streets he would watch rich people traveling in carriages, other people walking, and sometimes teamsters delivering goods in slow-moving carts. All these people seemed to be in a hurry, and this excited young Faraday—he felt more alive, more a part of this vibrant society. It felt refreshing to be on the streets because every step was an adventure, every block a new discovery. Here he was—a teenager—walking on the sidewalks of a world cultural and trade center! Michael could sense the excitement of the city—it was a place where anything could happen at any moment. Besides being a world port and the seat of the British Empire, London was the world's center of scientific activity. What a marvelous time to be alive!

Chapter 2

MICHAEL FARADAY,
BOOKBINDER'S APPRENTICE

After much hard work and many long hours talking with different employers, Michael landed a job on a trial basis as an errand boy for a man named Mr. Riebau. Riebau owned a bookbinding shop on Blandford Street that, besides binding books, loaned newspapers to selected customers. Not everyone bought a newspaper in the nineteenth century. Most people could not afford the price of one, so they borrowed papers in the same way that books are borrowed from a library today. Michael's job was to deliver these newspapers from one customer to another. He would wait until the customer finished reading the paper and then deliver the paper to the next customer. Michael liked to observe the events taking place around him as he worked, and he found that he learned almost as much from this as he did from reading books.

Michael also kept the shop clean and well maintained for Mr. Riebau. He swept the floor, dusted the bookshelves, washed windows, and, as a bonus for Mr. Riebau, often dusted the books.

Michael worked very hard as an errand boy for one full

year, then Mr. Riebau made Michael his apprentice. The apprenticeship would last for seven years, during which time Michael would live and work in Mr. Riebau's shop while he was learning the bookbinding trade. This was an exciting time for young Michael. He was learning how to assemble the pages of a book in their proper order, to sew the pages together, and to bind them with a leather cover. This may sound very simple, but it actually was very difficult. At that time, bookbinding was a very skilled trade that took years to learn. It was not easy to have every page of a book lie flat and then bind the pages together into a leather-bound volume.

Michael worked with other young men who were also apprenticing in Mr. Riebau's shop. Like Michael, they came from poor families while learning a trade. But it was Michael who really shone. He learned fast and soon was dextrous enough to sew pages together with little effort.

Michael was also different from the other boys in that he read every book he bound. It was as if he had a personal relationship with each manuscript. He read constantly in literature, science, and philosophy. Many times he would take down notes on what he had read, writing them down in much detail and somehow knowing that one day he would use the notes again. He believed that someday he would write a book of his own.

Michael kept his notes all over his room. Everywhere he turned he would find a piece of paper with some fact or statement written on it. His room was such a mess that he often could not find certain notes when he needed them. It was a problem that needed a solution, so Michael decided to compile his notes and then organize them into a notebook. He bound the notebook like a regular book and included an index in the front so that he could refer to any subject when he had a question.

Mr. Riebau also allowed Michael to make his bedroom a laboratory. Michael was introduced to electricity while reading the *Encyclopaedia Britannica*. Electricity fascinated him so much that he sought out more books and read everything he could find on the subject. Then he performed experiments to prove if what he had read was really true.

Michael read that electricity is a form of energy and that energy is the ability to do work. Michael became very interested in the concept of energy, or, more specifically, force. A force is a push or pull on an object, and Michael wondered what caused this push or pull. Where did energy come from? Why was it here? Is there an end to energy? All these questions, and many other like them, inspired Michael to develop his own ideas and theories. Because of Michael's readings and experiments with the idea of force he was able to make very important discoveries in electricity later in his life.

Michael also was fascinated with the concept of magnetism. He searched out and read all the literature available on the subject. He read that magnetism was originally discovered by the Greeks. First, there was amber, which is a hard, resinous substance that attracts light objects, such as feathers, paper, and hair. Later came the lodestone—magnetite—a substance that attracts iron objects.

The history of magnetism interested Michael as did the theories that explained how this strange phenomenon worked. After reading all about magnetism, Michael performed experiments in his room to test the ideas that he had read about. As always, he wrote down how he performed the experiment, his results, and then his conclusions. His early studies of magnetism and of force greatly influenced the development of Michael's theories on electricity.

One of the people that Michael respected most of all was Benjamin Franklin. From his readings Michael learned about Franklin's studies of electricity. Besides Franklin, Michael read about many other scientists and their pioneering discoveries in electricity. He read about Stephen Gray, an Englishman who discovered that some substances conduct electricity while others do not, and about Luigi Galvani, an Italian who experimented with electrical currents.

To Michael, however, the most exciting discoveries were those of Alessandro Volta, another Italian. Volta, a physicist, built the world's first battery, which he called a voltaic pile. Voltaic piles made it possible to have a steady source of electricity.

Michael liked to show Mr. Riebau his notebook in which he wrote down his experiments and notes. Mr. Riebau was quite impressed with Michael's work. He liked Michael and thought of him in a different way than he did his other apprentices. He often lent Michael books to read and introduced him to many interesting people. He knew that Michael would question these people, but it did not matter to Mr. Riebau. He wanted Michael to develop his ideas and his mind.

Mr. Riebau was so impressed with Michael's notebook that he asked if he could keep it for a while to read. Michael agreed. The next day Mr. Riebau showed the notebook to one of his customers, a man named Mr. Dance. Like Mr. Riebau, Mr. Dance was quite impressed with Michael's work, and he wanted to meet Michael. As they talked, Mr. Dance asked Michael if he had ever been to the Royal Institution to listen to the scientific lectures. Michael replied that he had not, and Mr. Dance was surprised. "A boy with your knowledge and talents shouldn't miss these lectures," he said. "There is a great opportunity for you to learn there." He told Michael that Sir Humphry Davy—who was one of England's greatest scientists—would soon speak at the Royal Institution, and he offered Michael tickets to the lecture.

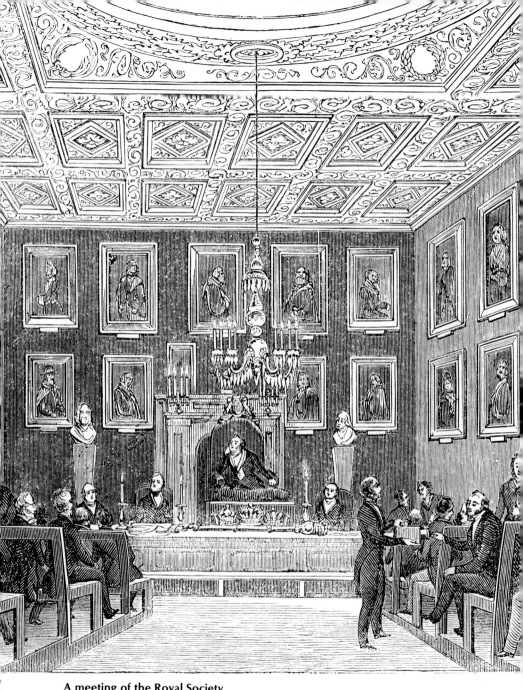

A meeting of the Royal Society

Chapter 3

MICHAEL FARADAY,
PHILOSOPHER AND SCIENTIST

Sir Humphry Davy made a big impression on young Michael Faraday. After receiving the tickets from Mr. Dance, Michael attended the lectures at the Royal Institution to hear Sir Humphry speak.

Michael took notes on the lectures, then he recopied his notes on clean paper and included drawings of the equipment that Sir Humphry used. He then bound the recopied notes together and made them into a thick book, which he studied to learn as much as he could.

Overwhelmed by the amount of information he had gathered from the four lectures given by Sir Humphry, Michael knew that there was so much more that he had to learn. He asked himself, "How can I do it? Where do I go next? Should I be a scientist and philosopher, or should I be a bookbinder?" These were difficult questions, and Michael was not sure that he had answers to them yet.

Soon after Sir Humphry Davy's lectures Michael joined the City Philosophical Society, a group that promoted scientific research and thought. Actually, the society was a "poor person's philosophical society." In the 1800s it was very difficult for a poor person to get an education, so the young people often met after the lectures to philosophize and to improve their speech, writing style, and dress.

For Michael, the City Philosophical Society was a marvelous opportunity to test his ideas on other people who thought the same way that he did. It was through the society that Michael gained the self-confidence to voice his own ideas.

It was important for Michael to meet other young men who were interested in science also. One of the men he met, Ben Abbott, became his good friend. Ben was younger than Michael (who was now nineteen), but they both shared a common interest in science. The two men rarely saw one another because they lived in different parts of London and because travel was difficult. But they maintained their friendship by writing letters.

Michael liked to write to Ben about his experiments. He would tell him where he bought his supplies and about the conversations he had with the suppliers, how he set up the experiment, and how he conducted the investigation.

Both Michael and Ben considered themselves philosophers. Most scientists of the nineteenth century considered themselves philosophers because they dealt with general laws of nature and the universe. Philosophy is the study of basic hypothesized truths (facts) and laws of the universe, and a philosopher is a person who studies, teaches, or writes about philosophy.

Michael considered himself a philosopher even before he finished his apprenticeship as a bookbinder. He believed that the way a person behaved defined that person as a philosopher. If you wanted to be a bricklayer, you laid bricks. If you wanted to be a philosopher, you philosophized or experimented with truths and laws.

The two books that influenced Michael most in his pursuit as a philosopher were the *Encyclopaedia Britannica* and Mrs. Marcet's *Conversations on Chemistry*. These books provided Michael with a solid foundation in science, and Michael believed that his studies of chemistry and electricity were an introduction to the study of philosophy.

Although Michael was an imaginative thinker who, like other young people, believed in fantasy, he was more influenced by facts. He could trust in facts and test them to prove or to disprove their validity. He discovered these facts about the world through his own experiments. He tested most things that interested him and developed his own philosophy of nature and the universe.

At this time Michael was greatly inspired by the lectures of John Tatum. Both Mr. Tatum and Sir Humphry gave lectures on science at the City Philosophical Society. These lectures were called "A Class on Perspective" and were sponsored by Mr. Tatum. Mr. Tatum's lectures increased Michael's knowledge of chemistry and physics.

Although Michael was an intelligent person and was bold enough to take steps to improve his life, he needed help from others to become the creative scientist he would soon become, and many people helped him.

James Faraday helped his son by answering Michael's questions, and this encouraged Michael to ask even more. Michael questioned his teachers, who were always busy with many students but who often took the time to answer him. It was only when Michael's questioning became too much that both his father and his teachers became frustrated providing answers.

Mr. Riebau greatly helped and influenced Michael. Not only did the bookbinder give the young man a job, but he provided an atmosphere in which Michael could learn and grow. Once Mr. Riebau discovered Michael's interest in science, he encouraged the young man's studies and experiments. Most important, the bookbinder also made it possible for Michael to meet people who might influence him. It was through Mr. Riebau that Michael became involved in the City Philosophical Society.

Mr. Tatum gave Michael his first opportunity to philosophize formally. He knew that it was difficult for poor young people to advance in English society. He gave them an opportunity to learn, study, and share their ideas with others. But it was Sir Humphry Davy whom Michael most admired and wanted to emulate.

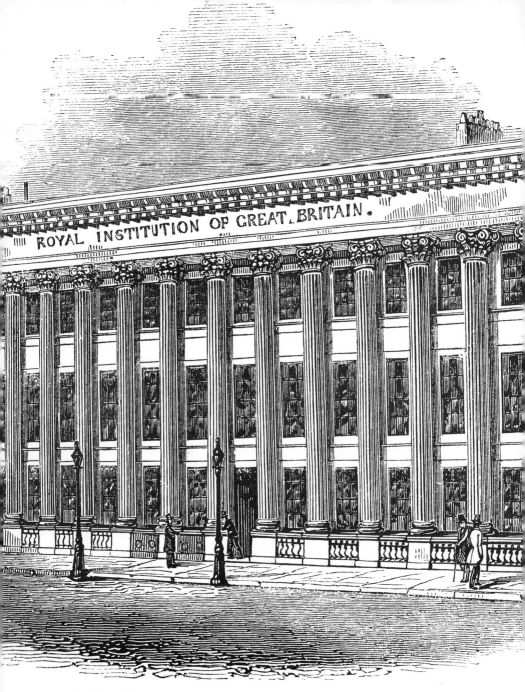

The Royal Institution

Chapter 4

THE ROYAL INSTITUTION

Michael Faraday was twenty-one years old when he successfully completed his bookbinder's apprenticeship. He was now a journeyman bookbinder. He had to leave his living quarters above Mr. Riebau's shop, and this was a crucial point in Michael's life because he had some very serious decisions to make. He was certain that he wanted to be a philosopher, yet he had spent all these years training to be a bookbinder. What should he do? He knew he had to get some advice.

Michael wrote to Ben Abbott, explaining his desire to be a philosopher and questioning whether he should take a chance at a career as a philosopher and scientist or pursue his career in bookbinding, for which he had trained a long time. Unfortunately, Ben had no answers.

Michael then questioned Mr. Riebau, who urged Michael to make up his own mind. He told Michael that he could be a success whatever decision he made. Still, though, Michael had doubts.

Until he made a final career decision, Michael decided to take a position as a bookbinder with a man named Mr. De la

Roche. Unlike Mr. Riebau, Mr. De la Roche was not sympathetic with Michael's career problems. Michael found it very unpleasant working for this man, so he became even more determined to become a philosopher.

Michael felt that trades such as bookbinding were harsh professions. He believed that most businesspeople were selfish and mean, whereas scientists were kind and gentle. A scientist-philosopher spent his or her time trying to help other people, not trying to take money away from them. Michael was more certain now than ever that he had to become a philosopher. He might even find a position at the Royal Institution.

The Royal Institution was founded in 1799 by Count Rumford. Its main purpose was to help the poor to improve their living conditions and to give them opportunities for advancement in society. At first Count Rumford's idea caught on, but after a short time the people rejected the project.

The Royal Institution continued, however, as a scientific society. During the 1800s, most scientific work was done by scientific societies. These societies were forerunners of today's universities. People employed in the societies were often called professors. The professors would give lectures, do research in laboratories, write papers, and publish their work in scholarly journals. The society paid the professors' salaries and sponsored their research. In return, the societies received the reputation for being progressive and humanitarian.

Sir Humphry Davy came to the Royal Institution in 1801. He was a brilliant speaker, scientist, philosopher, and poet, who had a great imagination and the ability to express himself well with words. Sir Humphry became very popular with the people of London, and he earned a reputation for his fantastic lecturing ability. More wealthy people now came to the Royal Institution, not so much to learn as to be entertained. Listening to Sir Humphry speak became a very popular thing to do in London.

Michael wrote a letter to Sir Humphry, asking him for a job at the Royal Institution. Faraday sent his notes that he had taken on Sir Humphry's lectures along with the letter, hoping that the notes would impress Sir Humphry.

Sir Humphry received Michael's letter and read it thoroughly. He was impressed with the young man's style and his courage in asking for a position. After reading the letter, Sir Humphry read the notes that Michael had taken. This impressed Sir Humphry even more. Who was this young man? he wondered. Why had he not heard of him before? He wanted to meet this man named Michael Faraday.

Months passed, and Michael still had not received an answer from Sir Humphry. He had been so hopeful when he had written. Mr. Dance had encouraged him to write. Mr.

Dance had said that Sir Humphry always was interested in talented young men. Had Mr. Dance been wrong? Perhaps Sir Humphry was too busy to bother.

Now things were worse than ever for Michael. He and Mr. De la Roche did not get along well. Because Michael had to earn a living, his dreams of becoming a philosopher and scientist seemed almost beyond reach. Michael tried to rationalize his situation as he resigned himself to being a bookbinder.

It was at this time that a series of events occurred that changed Michael's life. Late one night, when Michael was getting ready for bed at his mother's house, there was a knock on his door. Who could that be? he wondered. He knew that none of his friends would call this late in the evening.

Michael looked out from his bedroom window. He saw a very fancy carriage pulled by two sleek, gray horses. Michael knew that this type of carriage could be owned only by a wealthy person.

Michael put on his pants and went downstairs to open the door. Standing before him was a finely dressed footman, wearing a powdered wig. The footman smiled at Michael's astonished look and said, "Message for you, sir." He handed Michael an envelope, nodded, and went back to the carriage.

Michael sat down by the fireplace, opened the envelope,

and read the letter by the light of the glowing coals. The letter was from Sir Humphry Davy. He wanted to see Michael the next morning for an interview.

The next morning Michael put on his best clothes and went to the Royal Institution to meet with the great lecturer. Sir Humphry told Michael how impressed he had been with his letter and especially with his bound notebook. This showed him, Sir Humphry said, that Michael indeed did have the organization and discipline necessary to be a philosopher and scientist.

Sir Humphry said that science was a harsh master and that a career in this field, for most, was very frustrating. He told Michael that he was most likely better off being a bookbinder and that he was sorry, but at the present time there were no positions open at the Royal Institution. He would, however, keep Michael in mind if something opened up. Finishing up the interview, Sir Humphry told Michael that he would see to it that Michael's bookbinding company received all the work of the Royal Institution.

Michael was very disappointed. He thought Sir Humphry wanted to offer him a position at the Royal Institution, but now all his hopes were dashed. What did Sir Humphry call me in for anyway? What am I to do now? Am I really to be a bookbinder?

But Michael Faraday impressed Sir Humphry immensely. The scientist did not forget Michael, and several months later, when Sir Humphry was injured by an explosion in his laboratory, he sent for Michael to write letters for him. Soon after this, Sir Humphry asked Michael to become his assistant at the Royal Institution.

He could now leave Mr. De la Roche's shop. Michael had finally achieved one of his most important goals in life—he was now a laboratory assistant at the Royal Institution of London and working for Sir Humphry Davy, a dream come true!

Michael's first duty as Sir Humphry's assistant was to accompany him and his wife on a lecture tour of Europe. As they toured the continent, Michael had the chance to listen to all the lectures of Sir Humphry. He also was privileged to meet other great scientists of the time. In Paris, he met André Marie Ampère, the man who defined the relationship of forces between two wires carrying electric currents. This was an exciting time for Michael. Here he was touring Europe. Not bad for a man who came from such a poor background.

Although traveling through the continent of Europe was exciting and learning from Sir Humphry's lectures nice, Michael was not happy on this trip. It seemed to him that Sir Humphry's primary purpose for asking him along was to be a valet.

Michael had to carry the bags for Sir Humphry and his wife. He also ran errands, mailed letters, and carried books and packages. It was not so bad doing these things for Sir Humphry, but Mrs. Davy did not treat Michael respectfully, and Michael hated doing things for her. She would order Michael to do this or that; to pick up; to clean up; and she would not let Michael sit at the dinner table with her and Sir Humphry. This was very humiliating to Michael, especially when there were guests at dinner.

Michael became quite bitter. Many of his images were smashed by the reality of people's behavior. He saw that the great men of science were human, with human faults and mannerisms. They were not much different from the many businesspeople Michael had met while working for Mr. Riebau. He saw that many of the scientists had ego problems and that, in order to overcome their own insecurities, they considered themselves superior to others. Michael believed this was wrong. He believed that all people are equal.

Michael especially was disappointed in Sir Humphry. How could this great man let his wife, a bitter, scolding woman, run his life? It was at this time that Michael vowed he would never marry.

Michael and the Davys returned to London on April 23, 1815. It was a great day for Michael, for now he could get away from Mrs. Davy and get on with living his own life. He had a two-week vacation and then he went back to the Royal Institution, where he would continue as a laboratory assistant to Sir Humphry.

Michael earned thirty shillings a week (about thirty dollars a month), which was not a very large sum of money at that time. For that salary he had to work with Sir Humphry and help him with experiments and lectures, clean the laboratory, order equipment, repair broken equipment, and report any accidents (especially when equipment was broken) to the managers of the Royal Institution. But most of all, Michael liked assisting Sir Humphry in the laboratory. He would help set up the experiments, do the experiments, and, of course, clean up afterward.

Michael would describe the experiments in which he took part in letters to Ben Abbott. He would explain to Ben the things they were attempting to prove or disprove, how he and Sir Humphry would perform the experiments, and the results and conclusions of each experiment.

Many of the experiments that Sir Humphry and Michael performed were quite dangerous. Michael often described in letters to Ben Abbott the explosions that would occur and how lucky he was to have escaped injury. The young scientist seemed to think that he was protected from harm. He would perform dangerous experiments and, if an explosion occurred, would clean up, set up again, and start all over.

34

These were exciting years for Michael because he had done what few other people were able to. His dreams were becoming a reality. Here he was, actually practicing science and well on his way to becoming a full-fledged philosopher— and his mentor was Sir Humphry Davy.

Chapter 5

FARADAY'S EARLY YEARS AT THE ROYAL INSTITUTION: 1813-1821

Faraday was so busy with his work at the Royal Institution that he often missed meals. Many nights, after working very late on an experiment, he would fall asleep in the laboratory. He never had enough time because he had to clean up and maintain the equipment, then assist Sir Humphry at lectures. After all this, Michael would set up his own experiments and work on them very late into the evening. When he was finished, he would then have to log his results in his journal. There was never enough time.

Due to lack of sleep and the sore back he developed from sitting in the hard chairs in the laboratory, Faraday decided to move into the Royal Institution. He rented an attic room at the Institution and felt much better because he was closer to his work.

The room in which Faraday lived, learned, and experimented (yes, Faraday still performed experiments in his room, even though the laboratories of the Royal Institution were just downstairs) contained a desk, a bed, and some wooden chairs. It was not much, but for Faraday, who was not concerned with material things, it was more than enough. Faraday had what he wanted—a career in science and a chance to be a philosopher.

Faraday continued to write to Ben Abbott about all his experiences, but Ben's life was changing also. Ben had become quite involved with chemistry and then later switched his attention to electricity. This pleased Faraday. But around 1816 Faraday noticed that Ben was losing interest in science. It was at this time that Ben dropped all his studies in science. This saddened Faraday because Ben was one of the few persons in whom he confided.

In 1816 Faraday became a lecturer, giving a series of lectures to the members of the City Philosophical Society. Faraday was becoming well known among members of the scientific community. People respected his enthusiasm, his creativity, and his stubbornness. But Faraday's brilliance was not yet accepted—his originality was overshadowed by the reputation of Sir Humphry Davy. Not until later, when he and Sir Humphry went their separate ways, did people begin to recognize Faraday for his own genius.

Faraday spoke to the society on the research in chemistry and electricity being performed by Europe's scientists, in whom Faraday was disappointed. He felt that their opinions were biased, that they had lost their ability to think openly and creatively. The young scientist believed that people of science should be open-minded and willing to listen to all suggestions. Only after listening to and hearing all sides should they judge the evidence for themselves and make decisions. But to make decisions without hearing all the arguments, Faraday believed, was wrong. It was this type of idealism that characterized Faraday's life and that led Faraday, like most other idealists, to disappointment and humiliation. It seemed that setting high standards for humanity was a guarantee for failure.

Faraday believed that a scientist must free the imagination. Anything that one thought was an acceptable idea, but these thoughts and ideas had to be guarded by good judgment and principles. Even more important, these ideas had to be controlled and guided by experiment. If the idea did not hold up under strict experimentation, then the idea was not worthy of further investigation. People who did not subject their ideas to experiment were, in Faraday's opinion, false philosophers.

Faraday followed this philosophy in all his research. He truly believed that the human mind was limitless. He was not bound by the rules that prevented other scientists from creative discoveries. Faraday would experiment with most of the ideas that came into his mind, and because of this he is noted as one of history's most creative scientists.

Faraday attended church every Sunday. He belonged to a

small religious sect called the Sandemanians, and he felt very comfortable with these people. He liked their philosophy toward God and life.

It was in church that Faraday met Sarah Barnard. He was attracted to this quiet, dark-haired woman and liked her pleasant smile and sparkling eyes. Sarah was attracted to Faraday also. They often exchanged glances during service, but both Faraday and Sarah were shy people and did not make new acquaintances easily. It was several months before they actually spoke to one another. Then, by chance one day, they bumped into one another while leaving the service. Both of them were embarrassed at the face-to-face contact. Finally, Sarah broke the ice by smiling at Faraday. He returned her smile, then before they knew it they were talking with one another.

After their initial contact, the two met often after service. They would walk in the streets of London and talk. Faraday enjoyed this because Sarah would listen and seem to understand. He would spout his philosophies, and Sally (Faraday called her Sally) always seemed interested. She often encouraged him when he felt frustrated.

Soon Faraday began thinking about marrying Sally. He missed her when she was not with him. He would find himself often thinking of her while in the midst of an experiment. He felt that he wanted to be with her all the time, but what about his vow never to marry? Did he really want what Sir Humphry had? Still, Michael knew that Sally Barnard would never be like Mrs. Davy, so, in 1821, they got married.

FARADAY, MICHAEL

To develop his theories, Faraday had to test them.

Chapter 6

FARADAY DEVELOPS HIS THEORIES

Michael Faraday had an unusually strong desire to learn all about the physical world in which he lived. He developed his theory of matter while still living with Mr. Riebau. He believed that matter is anything that has weight and that takes up space. He also believed that matter was composed of force fields. In his adult years Faraday would speak about "the forces of matter," such as gravity.

While he was still a teenager, Faraday read that Dr. William Gilbert—an English physician who lived in the 1600s and who was often referred to as the father of magnetism—demonstrated that the Earth itself is a huge magnet. He studied the theories that explained how magnetism works and experimented with the Law of Poles, which states that all magnets have poles, or points, where their particular force is the strongest. These poles exert forces on one another. "Like" poles repel one another, while "unlike" poles attract one another.

Faraday learned that Earth's magnetic force, like other magnets, also is strongest at its poles. The Earth's magnetic poles attract the unlike poles of a magnet. This is why a compass needle always points to the north. A magnet's influence of attraction is called a force field.

Faraday's studies of magnetism led him to Benjamin Franklin's theories of electricity. Franklin was the first person to use the terms "positive" and "negative" when referring to electricity. Franklin believed that the positive forces of electricity repelled each other but that they attracted negative forces. It was not until the twentieth century that scientists learned that Franklin had confused the poles: what he had termed positive was negative, and what he had termed negative was positive. Franklin proved that lightning was charged with electricity in his kite experiment.

Faraday often wished that he had performed some of Luigi Galvani's experiments with frogs. Using copper hooks, Galvani attached the legs of frogs to a wet iron railing. The frogs' legs jumped and twitched when they touched the railing. Mistakenly, Galvani assumed that this indicated that frogs' legs contained electricity. Other scientists, however, proved Galvani wrong. They showed that electricity is not in living things, such as frogs' legs, but in the reactions of objects. For example, Galvani's frogs' legs twitched because of the actions between the copper hooks, iron railing, and moisture on the railing. The chemical action between these materials set up an electric current, which made the frogs' legs jump.

Most exciting to Faraday at this time, though, were Alessandro Volta's experiments with electricity. Volta created the voltaic pile, the world's first battery. The voltaic pile worked because of the chemical reactions between copper and zinc plates, which were separated by a cloth moistened in a salt solution. The steady source of electricity created by the voltaic pile is called an electromotive force (EMF). Electromotive force is the force that causes an electric current. In honor of Volta, electromotive force is commonly measured in units called volts.

Faraday also admired Sir Humphry Davy for his far-reaching experiments in electricity. In 1801 Sir Humphry discovered the electric arc, a current of electricity that would jump between two carbon rods. This arc was the prototype of the arc lamp. Sir Humphry also built the world's largest battery.

When Mr. Dance introduced Faraday to the Royal Institution, Faraday read about the experiments of the institution's founder, Count Rumford. Count Rumford was interested in heat, and he performed many experiments to discover the origins of it. He eventually proved that rubbing one object against another causes friction.

The study of science in areas such as magnetism, electricity, and chemistry fascinated Faraday. It was often difficult for him to decide on which subject he wanted to concentrate next. Throughout his lifetime he would spend long periods of time studying many different areas of scientific research and experimentation.

Faraday spent his first years at the Royal Institution delving into chemistry. He performed experiments in electrolysis and the liquefaction of gases. Sir Humphry was involved in electrolysis. He and Faraday did many experiments together, and Sir Humphry discovered the existence of elements that had never before been isolated. Today's liquefied gases that are fuel for rocket engines are made by the same process that Faraday discovered in the nineteenth century.

The year 1820 marks the time when Faraday, at the age of twenty-nine, left the study of chemistry to return to the study of electricity. This change was stimulated by Hans Oersted, a Danish scientist who had been doing some research with magnetism and electricity.

In 1819 Oersted discovered that an electric current, passing through a conductor (wire), deflects the needle of a compass. In essence, the current of electricity creates a magnetic field. Each time a current was passed through the wire or was stopped, the compass needle changed direction.

Sir Humphry, as well as Faraday, was excited about Oersted's discovery. Sir Humphry insisted that both he and Faraday work on this new idea in their laboratory at the Royal Institution. The two scientists laid a compass down on a board and wrapped several turns of electrical wire around the compass and the board. The wire was then connected to a battery. When the current was connected to the compass, the needle jumped in one direction. When the current was disconnected, the needle jumped in the opposite direction.

FARADAY'S EXPERIMENT IN ELECTROMAGNETISM

As current (the arrows) passed over the compass, the needle of the compass would jump.

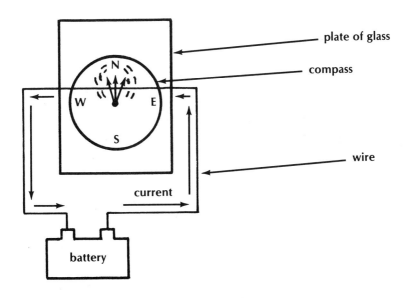

Faraday was fascinated by the interaction of electricity and magnetism. During the weeks and months that followed, he kept returning to Oersted's experiment, performing it over and over again. Each time he recreated the experiment, he analyzed the results. Why, he asked himself, does the compass needle jump in one direction when the battery is connected to the wire, then, when the wire is disconnected, move in the other direction?

Faraday read and reread Oersted's work, studying the Dane's theory on electrical rotation. Oersted believed that an electrical current—the flow of electricity through a conductor or transmitter—caused circles of force around a wire. This was based on Ampère's Law, which states that the magnetic force of an electric current gives the direction of the force as always being around the wire. This assumed that the force did not go toward or away from the wire.

Faraday's curiosity was piqued by Oersted's research and by his own experiments, so he wrote a paper entitled "History of the Progress of Electromagnetism." In this paper and through his experiments Faraday began to question Oersted's and Ampère's theories. Faraday wondered, If there were circles of force around a wire, why would the same not be true for a magnet? If this premise was true, then why would objects not move in circles around a magnet?

Faraday decided to investigate the possibilities of producing a rotation by magnetic interaction. Faraday's unique idea was that an electric current could produce rotation (circular motion) of a magnet's poles around a conducting wire.

Faraday envisioned an electrically charged wire that could freely move around a magnet, so he began to set up this experiment. He arranged a magnetic needle upright in a glass tube. The glass tube stood upright in a cup of mercury with a wire hanging from a pivot above. The magnet was secured with paraffin wax, which was surrounded by the mercury in the cup. The end of the pivoted wire was dipped into the mercury and was free to move in a circle around the poles of the magnet.

With this apparatus in place, an electric current was then passed through the wire, the circuit being completed by the mercury. Faraday believed that, when the circuit was completed, the conducting wire would be driven in a circle around the magnet.

On September 3, 1821, Faraday made the great discovery. His brother-in-law, George Barnard, was in the laboratory with him and Sally. Faraday hooked one wire to the powerful battery made by Sir Humphry. This wire led to the coil that held the pivoting needle. Then he hooked the wire to the battery, and the wire's end was suspended in the mercury.

FARADAY'S FIRST SUCCESSFUL ATTEMPT, 1821 — ELECTRIC MOTOR

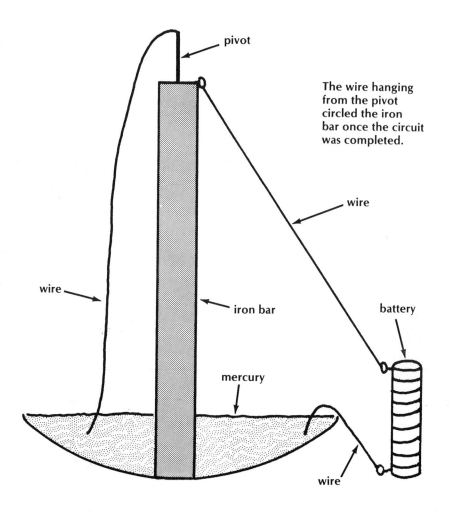

pivot

The wire hanging
from the pivot
circled the iron
bar once the circuit
was completed.

wire

wire

iron bar

battery

mercury

wire

The circuit was complete. The wire began to revolve around the magnet.

Faraday had proved that the magnetic force field—the space around a magnet—will make an electrified wire move in a circle around the magnet's pole. It is the push and pull (force) of the magnet's field that makes the wire move. As the Law of Poles states: Unlike poles attract one another, while like poles repel one another.

The electrically charged wire has magnetic properties—it acts like a magnet. The poles of the wire are repelled by the like poles of the magnet and, therefore, cause the wire to move away. This repulsion is what causes the rotation.

Faraday's experiment was a giant step forward in the progress of electrical science. He did not know it then, but his discovery of electromagnetic rotation was the forerunner of the electric motor. In the years to come, other inventors would use his discoveries to build efficient electric motors that would run all sorts of electrical devices.

Michael Faraday's discoveries were unique and original. He was excited about his discoveries, so he recorded everything he did in his journal. Here he also discussed the ideas that led to his discoveries, the experiments themselves, the results, and his conclusions. Faraday published the findings of his experiments, but immediately he was accused of being a plagiarist.

It was Sir Humphry who accused Faraday of plagiarism. Faraday had advanced over the years and surpassed Sir Humphry in his knowledge of electrical science. Sir Humphry was jealous of Faraday and his achievements, so he accused Faraday of stealing the discovery of electromagnetic rotation from William Hyde Wollaston, a chemist and metallurgist who was working on electromagnetism at the same time as Faraday.

In 1821 Faraday was nominated to become a fellow of London's famed Royal Society. Sir Humphry asked Faraday to withdraw his name because he thought Faraday was not ready for membership. When Faraday refused, Sir Humphry became furious. Their friendship ended at this time.

Sir Humphry's charges and accusations proved to be false, so Faraday was cleared of any charges of plagiarism, and his reputation was saved. The truth was that, while both Michael Faraday and William Wollaston had been working on the same principle, Faraday's experiments worked, and Wollaston's did not. Faraday's experiments, although similar to Wollaston's, were uniquely his own. Sir Humphry was forced to drop the charges he had made against Faraday.

The entire affair took over two years to work itself out. During this time, Faraday, a sensitive person, was emotionally scarred and became bitter and withdrawn. He became distrustful of people and avoided most social contacts. He remained friendly only with his close relatives. Faraday also avoided accepting awards or honors, such as the knighthood that the British government wished to bestow on him.

Faraday, like a turtle in its shell, stayed in his laboratory and became even more involved in research. He gave up the study of electricity and concentrated his efforts in other areas. He worked with glass, attempting to make better lenses, and with various kinds of metals, trying to make them stronger.

Faraday working in his laboratory at the Royal Institution

Chapter 7

A CHANGE OF PACE FOR FARADAY

In 1825 Faraday was appointed director of the laboratory at the Royal Institution. Along with this promotion he received a raise in his salary to one hundred pounds per year (then about five hundred dollars), plus a house, coals for heat, and candles for light. Since Faraday was not mainly interested in making money, he was happy with his raise and most likely would have taken the job without it.

Sally, too, was not a pretentious person. It was just the two of them, so what else did they need? They did not travel much or go out, and they did not often entertain guests. The Faradays were happy with their lives.

As director of the laboratory, Faraday became a consultant for the courts, who would call on him from time to time to give his expert testimony in legal cases involving lawsuits against various companies. One such company was a coal company in Haswell, which had a huge explosion in one of its mines. Many people had been hurt, and some were killed. No one knew what caused the explosion, but the company and the people of Haswell were determined to prevent similar accidents.

After questioning some of the miners and their managers, Faraday concluded that the explosion was caused by gunpowder, which had been used for various tasks while mining. The people of the mine had stored the gunpowder in large bags in the mines, so Faraday's recommendation was that the gunpowder be stored in a safe container in a safe place.

Faraday also lectured more than ever before. As director, he was expected to lecture, and this he truly loved. He spoke at the Royal Institution and for other clubs and civil groups.

Because of his own experiences as a youth, and because he remembered how strong was his desire to learn, Faraday believed that the Royal Institution should do something to sharpen children's interest in science and to satisfy their curiosity. It was this belief that inspired him to lecture to children during the Christmas holiday, when they were free from school.

The children would jam the auditorium at the Royal Institution to hear Faraday speak. As he stood at the podium and looked out at the young audience, he was reminded of his youth. There were children with notebooks, ready to write down every word he said, while others were there just to listen. Perhaps there was a young inventor out there who, through the lectures, would be inspired to pursue a career as a philosopher.

Faraday's lectures covered all aspects of science. He would talk about the forces of matter, the unlimited experiences in science, and the wonders of the universe. His most famous lecture to the children was entitled "The Chemical History of a Candle." During this lecture, in a darkened auditorium, Faraday would light a candle, then ask questions about the candle and answer them. The children loved this lecture, and, because it was so popular, Faraday included it in every Christmas lecture series. The lectures were a nice change of pace for Faraday, but his first love was still his research and philosophy.

A blacksmith of the nineteenth century

Bookbinders at work in the mid-nineteenth century

Two scenes of Michael Faraday's London

Faraday lecturing at the Royal Institution

Faraday and his wife Sally

Benjamin Franklin

Volta demonstrating the voltaic pile

Sir Humphry Davy

A statue of Faraday in the hall of the Royal Institution

Chapter 8

FARADAY'S GREATEST DISCOVERY

Most of Faraday's discoveries are related to his idea of matter. Matter is anything that has weight and that occupies space. An object (matter)—any object—is not affected by the forces of other objects but by its own forces. All objects on Earth are matter. According to Faraday, all objects are fields of force. It is the interaction of each object's individual force with another's that causes electricity.

In making the electric motor Faraday put his theories to the test. The pivot wire, over the magnet, is the center of its own force. The magnet is also the center of its own force. When the electric current is passed through the wire, the forces of the wire interact with the forces of the magnet. This is the Law of Poles in action. The wire's positive forces are repelled by the magnet's positive forces while attracted to the magnet's negative forces. It is this interaction—the attraction and the repulsion—that causes the wire to move in a circular motion around the magnet.

These thoughts were the beginning of Faraday's Field Theory, his ideas on fields of force. Faraday was one of the first scientists to challenge Newton's ideas of forces. Sir

Isaac Newton's Laws of Gravitational Forces states that forces can act only on objects. For example, the force of gravity acts on every object on Earth. Faraday said that this was not so, that forces act on forces and not on objects.

In the 1820s most English scientists ignored Faraday's refutation of Newton's theories and called Faraday's ideas outlandish and dangerous, even revolutionary. Non-English scientists, however, praised Faraday's work, calling him one of the finest authorities in physics and electromagnetics in the world.

Faraday believed in what his research showed him. He was not one to put forth ideas without evidence. His philosophy was that facts come first, then, from these facts, theories are constructed. For Faraday it was obvious from the facts that were revealed in his electric-motor experiment that Newton was wrong. Because the scientists did not trust his studies, Faraday continued with his research.

Each time he performed his electric-motor experiment, Faraday came up with more evidence to back up his findings. He postulated that lines of force were always present and that all forces were forces of matter. He also believed that every force could convert to every other force. All magnetic and electric forces move in space, he stated. All forces can be changed to other forces because all things are made up of force fields.

Faraday wrote all his ideas down on paper. He published his ideas, experiments, and findings in scholarly papers and journals. Initially, Faraday had been known as a chemist and metallurgist, and it was only after he published his ideas on electricity that he became respected as a physicist.

Although Faraday's success at consulting was very gratifying to him, many of his disagreements with the scientific community continued during the 1820s. For example, Faraday believed in the conservation of matter, the theory that forces can be transferred or converted to other forces. This idea was in opposition to that of Alessandro Volta.

Volta believed that his voltaic pile worked by the principle of contact electricity. Contact electricity means that electricity is produced because of the metals and chemicals being in contact with one another, but Faraday disagreed. He said that if Volta's pile did do this, it would be producing energy for nothing.

Faraday hypothesized that energy cannot be created or destroyed but that it can be transferred and transformed. As an example, if the energy in Volta's pile came from the metals, he wondered, why was it not used up and why were the metals still intact? The answer, for Faraday, was that energy did not come from the metals. He insisted that the chemical action between the metals in the pile was a force that acted on another force and was not merely the contact of different substances. He also insisted that, when the chemical action wore down or was used up, the electricity ceased. This argument continued for years until, finally, Faraday's theory was proven correct.

Other people were also involved in electrical research. A Frenchman named Dominique Arago discovered that the swings of a pivoted magnetic needle slowed down when it was brought close to a sheet of copper. What did this mean? Arago also discovered that a disc of metal would pull a magnet around with it as the disc rotated. Why? These were questions that plagued Faraday as he read about the research of other scientists.

An Englishman named William Sturgeon produced the first electromagnet in 1825. An electromagnet is a magnet that works by an electrical current being passed around it. A piece of iron is wrapped in wire, and, when the electric current goes through the wire, it makes an electromagnet out of the iron.

Sturgeon's magnet was a piece of iron that was bent into a horseshoe shape and wrapped with sixteen turns of a wire, each turn being separated from the other. When a current was passed through the wire, the magnet could support objects that weighed as much as nine pounds.

Faraday found Sturgeon's experiments fascinating. This—along with Sir Humphry Davy's observation that a

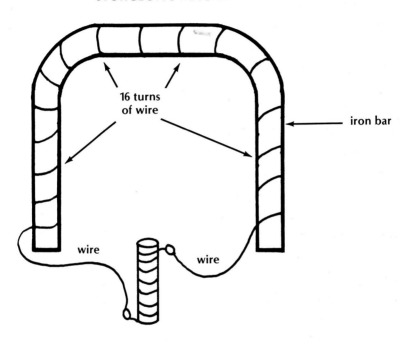

16 turns
of wire

iron bar

wire

wire

copper wire with an electric current passing through it
would attract iron filings—made Faraday believe even more
strongly that magnetism could produce electricity.

Faraday performed more electrical experiments and continued his lecturing, consulting, and chemistry. Most of his
time was spent on chemistry and metallurgy now, but he
was still bothered by the problem of proving that electricity

could be produced from magnetism if magnetism could be produced from electricity.

The correctness of Faraday's premise was supported by all the research at that time. After all, he knew that everything in nature and the universe has a counterpart. It is this balance of the natural world that convinced Faraday that his ideas were sound. Newton had said that there is action and a reaction. Faraday knew that the chemical action in a battery would produce electricity and that electricity would produce the chemical action. Everything in the world affects every other thing, and they are all affected by one another. Thus, he reasoned, if magnetism can be produced by electricity, then electricity can be produced by magnetism.

The idea of electromagnetic induction—the production of electricity from magnetism—kept coming to Faraday, so he began to do more experiments to prove his theory. Eventually, he gave up his experiments in optics and worked only on electromagnetic induction.

Faraday experimented for months, attempting to create successfully electricity from magnetism. First, he set up an elaborate apparatus made up of a wooden spool that was wound with twelve spirals of wire and insulated by calico and twine. He connected the even-numbered coils into a series and the odd-numbered coils into another series. He connected one set to a battery and the other set to a galvanometer.

FARADAY'S FIRST ATTEMPT AT INDUCTION

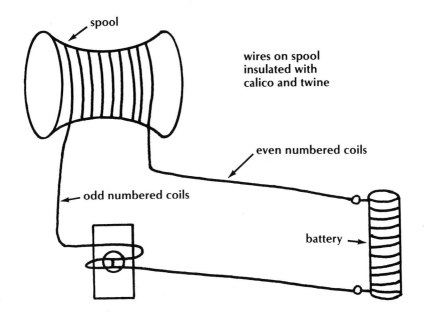

On his first attempt with this setup, Faraday saw no effect on the galvanometer. Not being one to give up easily, he analyzed the results of this first attempt and inferred that the equipment failed because he did not use a powerful enough battery. So the scientist tried again, this time using a much more powerful battery. Though the current flowed through the wires, there was still no noticeable effect on the galvanometer; but, when the current was disconnected and the current broken, the needle of the galvanometer deflected.

Faraday performed the experiment again. This time he noticed that the galvanometer deflected when the circuit was first made and when it was broken. These deflections in the galvanometer were so small that it was a wonder that Faraday even noticed them. What this experiment showed was that, when there was no current, or no steady current, in the battery coil, there was no induced electricity; but when the current was started or stopped, there was induced electricity. For the first time ever, an electric current had been produced through magnetic interaction.

Faraday analyzed the results of his experiment. Why did this happen? What caused the induced current? He reasoned that the electricity was always produced when there was a change in the lines of magnetic force. It was the production of the lines of force and the lack of production that caused the current in a nearby circuit. In other words, as long as the lines of force were constant, no current could be produced in a nearby circuit, but, when the lines of force were created or stopped, an electric current was induced in a nearby circuit. This was the start of Electromagnetic Theory.

On December 17, 1831, Faraday perfected his experiment on induced current by adding a hollow spiral to his apparatus, replacing the wound iron coil. He connected this helix parallel to a galvanometer. He then put a bar magnet into the hollow of the helix and got immediate results on the galvanometer. When he withdrew the magnet from the helix, he again got results on the galvanometer. All the time that the bar magnet remained in the cylinder, there was no reading on the galvanometer.

Faraday continued to experiment and to perfect the induction of electricity. He wanted to be able to generate a constant electrical current. He attempted this by placing a copper disc on an axle with wires touching the edge of the disc and the axle, then connecting the wires to the galvanometer. The disc was situated between two poles of a powerful horseshoe magnet. When the disc was rotated, an electric current was induced.

Faraday wrote down how he set up and performed his experiments. In November 1831 he reported his results to the Royal Society. In his paper he developed two laws from his experiments:

> 1. When the flow of magnetic induction through a circuit is changing, an electromotive force (the force that pushes electric current) is induced in the circuit.
> 2. The strength of this electromotive force is directly proportional to the rate of change in the flow of magnetic induction.

FARADAY'S GENERATOR

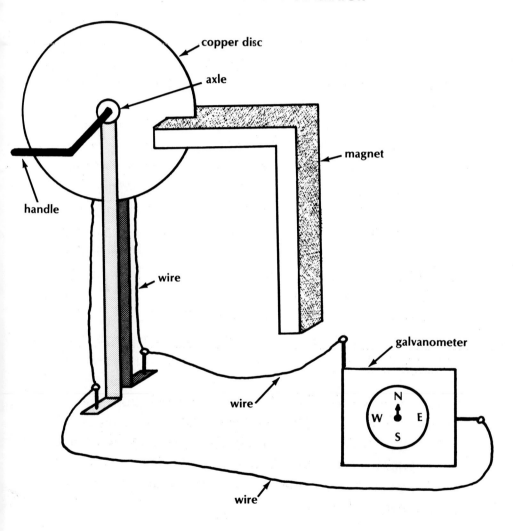

In other words, a magnet induces an electric current, and the amount of current is determined by how fast or slow the magnet changes the fields of force.

The scientists of the Royal Society accepted Faraday's work with great interest. He had invented the electric generator, or dynamo. This discovery has made a great impact on the world, and it was Faraday's greatest contribution. Today, more electricity is produced by Faraday's methods than by any other means. Yes, there are other ways of producing electricity, such as with thermocouples, which produce electricity by using heat; with photoelectric cells, which produce electricity by using light; and with batteries. All these methods are used today, but all the others combined do not come near to equaling the amount produced by Faraday's generator.

It seems that many of the great discoveries in science have been made by more than one person who was working on the same idea independently of another. This is not so surprising if you consider that the research is based on where the state of the art is at the present time. In the 1800s people were fascinated by electricity and magnetism. Papers were published every month that told of new discoveries or that offered new interpretations of old discoveries. Is it any wonder that more than one person could be working on the same idea?

For example, in Albany, New York, a man named Joseph Henry worked with electromagnetism at about the same time that Faraday worked on his generator. Henry built electromagnets by winding coils around iron cores and called them intensity magnets. After a while, Henry wondered if it were possible to operate an electromagnet at a distance. This was the first step toward the concept of a telegraph, but unfortunately Henry never followed through on this idea.

Eventually, Henry arrived at the idea of electromagnetic induction. He experimented with this idea at the same time that Faraday was working on his experiments on electricity. Unlike Faraday, Henry did not keep good records of his work, and he also did not write scholarly papers.

When Faraday published his paper in 1831, the scientific world accepted him as the discoverer of electromagnetic induction. Joseph Henry himself credited Faraday with this discovery. But Henry is credited with the discovery of self-induction, which is the event of a second current moving in the opposite direction of the dying-out current. To honor Henry for his discovery, the self-inductance of a circuit is measured in units called henrys.

Faraday also has electricity measurements named after him. He is the only scientist to have two such units ascribed to his name. The size of electric condensers is measured in farads, and the amount of electricity with a certain chemical effect is called a faraday.

Michael Faraday's discovery of electromagnetic induction paved the way for changing mechanical energy into electrical energy. This important principle is based on the First Law of Thermodynamics.

Faraday had come up with a new idea of energy. He discovered that the movement of a magnet caused a current in a wire. The movement is mechanical energy, and, when this movement causes current, it is converted to electrical energy. Faraday's experiment proved that a current is the result of the motion of a conductor interacting with a magnetic field.

Faraday's disc experiment turned out to be the first direct-current dynamo. It was the first device to change mechanical energy into a steady electric current.

Electric generators today, based on Faraday's experiment conducted over 150 years ago, power the world. Generators that are run by water power (hydroelectric power), coal, oil, and nuclear energy provide electric power.

All the generators work on the principle of converting mechanical energy into electrical energy. This electrical energy goes out from the power station and is again converted into other forms of energy when it reaches the homes, businesses, and industries that use it.

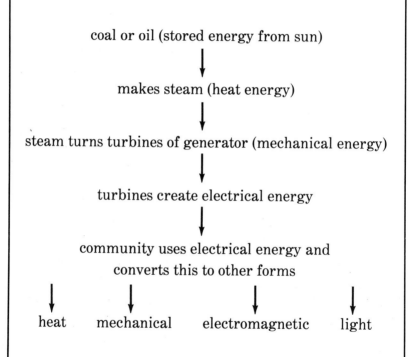

POWER PLANT TO COMMUNITY SCHEMATIC

coal or oil (stored energy from sun)
↓
makes steam (heat energy)
↓
steam turns turbines of generator (mechanical energy)
↓
turbines create electrical energy
↓
community uses electrical energy and
converts this to other forms

↓   ↓   ↓   ↓

heat   mechanical   electromagnetic   light

Chapter 9

THE YEARS AFTER

Often a great discovery is the most distinctive part of a person's life, and the time after becomes an anticlimax. This was not so with Michael Faraday. Although Faraday's greatest discoveries were made in the early 1800s, he continued to progress in his work and contribute to humanity. He strived to find solutions for many questions that were not yet answered. He consolidated his research in a three-volume work, *Experimental Researches in Electricity*, and continued his lectures for the public.

Faraday was respected throughout the world. His discoveries were read and accepted by scholars in most nations of the western hemisphere. Along with this acceptance came invitations to speak, requests for advice, and offers of consultative positions.

Most people would have been extremely pleased. Each of us wants to be recognized for our efforts, especially if those struggles represent a lifetime of work. Yet Faraday was reluctant. He shunned the fame that accompanied his success. Many times the scientist would reflect back on his childhood and his family's struggle for survival. He would ask himself, Are things really that different now? Am I not the same person now as I was then? He felt unable to accept many of the honors that were bestowed on him by the government and various private groups.

Faraday was offered the presidency of the Royal Society, the same institution that, not many years before, would not allow him to be a member, but he refused the offer. He was asked to be president of his beloved Royal Institution, and again he refused. He was afraid that taking the presidencies would pull him away from his research, and he could not allow this to happen. His first love was his research. He still asked many questions, much as he did when a small child, and attempted to discover everything that he could about the world.

Besides, Faraday felt that being president of the Royal Society or the Royal Institution would push Sally and him into the social circle of "high society." They would have to attend parties and dinner affairs with rich people, all the time politicking for the benefit of the Royal Institution. He would be surrounded by rich people, people seeking favors, or people who hoped to enhance their own reputation by being close to him.

This was not the life for Michael Faraday. He preferred the simple life and was often embarrassed by his fame. He wanted to be only an ordinary British citizen. This is why he refused England's offer of knighthood. "I have lived my life as a plain person," he said, "and I shall die as a plain person."

As his discoveries became better known and his reputation enhanced, Faraday became more and more withdrawn. He began to refuse speaking engagements, and, after a time, he gave up all his speaking appearances, except for those at the Royal Institution and his Christmas lectures for the children. He loved the children. They were so anxious to learn, and this reminded him of his own childhood curiosity. It was so simple and honest.

Occasionally, Faraday also gave free lectures for the British government. He believed that this was his duty as a citizen. He was committed to lecturing at the Woolwich Military Academy, where he spoke to young officers on how a science background could make them better officers. He also served as a consultant to Trinity House on the maintenance of lighthouses and worked with the British Port Authorities on methods for improving the lighting of the harbors.

In avoiding publicity, while still attempting to perform his research, Faraday grew closer to and more dependent on Sally. He looked to her to protect him from the public as well as to nurture him at home. He enjoyed sharing quiet moments with his wife. Often he would persuade her to refuse dinners or other social engagements so that the two of them could stay home alone. There they would sit in front of the fireplace and share a book. He would prattle about his research as she listened attentively.

It was fortunate for Faraday that he had Sally because she understood him. While many wives of famous men, such as Mrs. Davy, would press their husbands to accept the honors bestowed on them, Sally did not. Sally knew that Faraday needed his privacy. She herself was not anxious to be in the public eye, and she made an effort to give Faraday what he needed most: a quiet, peaceful home where he could relax and hide from the world that continually sought him out.

Still, with their desire for seclusion, the Faradays' lives were not dull. Faraday was very active in his research and would spend all day in his laboratory working on various projects in chemistry, metallurgy, and electricity. Sally was also very busy. She was active in her church, and she was always busy with church and charitable activities. Also, they both loved the theater.

In 1831, when Faraday discovered electromagnetic induction, he found that his life was growing far too complicated. To combat this and to give himself more time, he gave up his private consulting practice. This was a decision that was not made lightly because, in giving up this practice, he also gave up the large income he received from the Royal Institution and some savings that they had accumulated over the years. But now he had more time to spend in his laboratory working on his research and more time to be with Sally.

Faraday also became more involved in his writing and philosophy. It was during the years 1832-34 that the scientist reflected on his past research and developed his world view. His philosophy involved the three major areas of his research: force, conservation of force, and field theory.

It was Faraday's philosophy and methods of scientific investigation that separated him from the rest of the scientific community. Unlike other scientists of the time, Faraday's fresh and revolutionary ideas were formed from sound, step-by-step research and investigation. He did not attempt to fool others about his methods of discovery, and, therefore, he always detailed everything he did to reach a discovery. It was this honesty that made him different from his colleagues.

Many other famous scientists of the time hid the methods of their investigations. Newton, Ampère, and others merely revealed their findings but not their methods. Faraday had a problem with this. He believed that the way a person came to a discovery was often more important than the discovery itself.

Another disagreement that Faraday had with his colleagues was that of philosophy. For a person to be a true philosopher, Faraday proclaimed, that person must free his or her mind of any prejudiced or bigoted thoughts. How could one think freely if the mind was in chains? There was no idea so sacred that it could not be challenged. It was the duty of a philosopher to challenge accepted ideas and, in doing so, help the world to grow and change. Faraday believed that anyone who could resist prejudice could be as successful as he was.

False scientists, or pseudoscientists, is what Faraday called researchers who were prejudiced in their beliefs. They do not enter the field of investigation hoping to uncover bold, new concepts, but they enter instead to prove or verify their own preconceived theories. They do not use the scientific method of discovery in solving problems. Instead of stating a problem to be solved, the pseudoscientists start with an experiment that is designed to prove what they want to happen. Faraday held the idea that a scientist should start with the problem, put the problem in the form of a hypothesis, and then prove or disprove the hypothesis by experiment. He believed that experimentation would rule out, by concrete evidence, any preconceived prejudices.

It was because Faraday refused to be controlled by ideas of the past that he was able to develop his philosophy on the conservation of force. This was a bold and revolutionary idea and was rejected by many of the scientists of the time. Still,

Faraday insisted that his thoughts were correct, and time has shown that he indeed was right.

It was his unique view of science and life that made Faraday so different from other scientists of his time. As he researched and wrote about the work of other scientists, Faraday would point out their failures as well as their great discoveries. He pointed out the legitimate developments that the scientists made toward their discoveries. Faraday's style as a scientist was new. People had an image of scientists as unable to err, and if they should err, then it must be because their ideas were wrong. Faraday did not believe this—he felt that all people made mistakes, including scientists.

Faraday set down his philosophy and experiments in the three books entitled *Experimental Researches in Electricity*. In these volumes, a step-by-step account is given on how the scientist goes about performing his experiments and reaching his conclusions. These were so well written that even Faraday's enemies had to admit to the greatness of his work.

As the years passed, Faraday's personality gradually seemed to change, and he often appeared giddy and forgetful. These fits of giddiness came on him suddenly. Many times Sally would have to rescue him from embarrassing situations. People just would not understand, and she knew that. She was afraid that they would think Faraday was crazy or that he was becoming senile.

87

As these fits became more frequent, Faraday grew unhappy. What was happening to him? Was he losing control? He was embarrassed to be among people because he never knew when he would behave inappropriately. Would someone ask him a question on his work that he would not be able to answer? This would be awful and unacceptable for such a proud man.

To avoid these confrontations, Faraday withdrew even further. Sally often could not break through this wall that he built around himself. Still, though, he continued to grow more depressed and to become more irritable and irrational as the fits of giddiness and forgetfulness visited more often. Finally, in 1845, when Faraday was fifty, he suffered a nervous breakdown.

Totally unable to function, Faraday was forced to give up his work for complete bed rest. The doctor ordered him not to think about his scientific work or his philosophizing. He was told to clear his mind of all thoughts except those of getting well. He was warned that, although he may feel better, he actually was not and that going back to work would surely push him to another breakdown that would be worse than the first.

This tremendous tragedy tore at Faraday's soul. Had it not been for Sally's love and dedication, the scientist probably would not have recovered from his illness. As it was, recovery took a long time—an almost endless time for Faraday.

Sally did her best to occupy Faraday so that he would not feel sorry for himself. They made frequent visits to the London Zoo. Faraday was a member of the Zoological Society. Both of them loved animals. Faraday was especially fond of the monkeys. He would watch them and often think how much they behaved like humans. Are we, he questioned, that much different from them?

Sally tried to convince her husband that they should move out of their apartment at the Royal Institution. They should leave London and live in the country, she said. Faraday would not hear of this. How could he leave? This was his home. He thought that, even though he could not work now, he would be able to soon. What would happen when he was well again? If they left the Royal Institution, where would they live when he was researching again?

Since Faraday would not move, Sally found other things to interest him besides his work. They would go to plays and the opera. Often they would watch the puppet shows of Punch and Judy. On the streets of London, Faraday was entertained by acrobats, magicians, and dwarfs.

Faraday also enjoyed the company of his two nieces. They would come to visit, and he would demonstrate experiments. The girls were delighted by their uncle's work. Often they would all sit by the fire and read together.

This was good for Faraday because he felt part of a bigger family. It was a quiet respite from his illness.

When things got really bad with Faraday's illness, Sally would insist that they leave London for a while and travel in the country. She and the doctor believed that a change of environment would do the scientist a great deal of good.

Faraday would often get upset with his doctors, especially at times when his recovery was not progressing. "They use fancy words," he would say, "but what they really want is for me not to work. They don't want me to talk, to work, to think. What can I do?"

However, Michael Faraday was a very strong person. His personality was such that he would not, could not, give up. Slowly, he started to get better and, eventually, to get back to his work. It was only with the greatest effort that he overcame his illness. However, although Faraday now appeared well, he was constantly struggling and pushing himself to achieve. It was not that he was cured. No, he believed he was stronger than the illness that plagued him.

Faraday did some of his best work after returning from his illness. It was Faraday's theories on force that led him to his discoveries on the effects of magnetism on light. He believed that all objects exert force on other objects and that this force can be exerted from a distance. However, in order for the force to be effective at a distance, it has to utilize the empty space that is between the two objects. For example, a tugboat can pull another boat to dock, but without a tow line between the two boats, the tugboat's force becomes ineffective.

Applying the tugboat principle to his research with light, Faraday gave his own unique definition to the idea of light being an all-pervasive force, known as an aether. Most scientists at that time believed that there were two aethers, one for light and another for electricity, but Faraday disagreed. He believed that light and electricity, if aethers really existed, were part of the same aether and that they affected each other. As his theory of aethers developed, Faraday concluded that aethers did not exist other than as fields of force, namely, as an electromagnetic force field.

Faraday investigated his theories of aethers as fields of force. In November 1845 he announced the results of his experiments in a paper entitled *Magnetization of Light and the Illumination of the Lines of Magnetic Force.* This was a revolutionary breakthrough in field theory. It explained how electromagnetic force fields can polarize light waves.

Faraday knew that, in order to polarize light, the vertical light waves must be blocked from the horizontal light waves. He observed that a magnetic force field, when parallel to a ray of light, would cause a change in the direction in the vibrations of the light waves. This connection between light and magnetism, and the effects of magnetism on light, was one of Faraday's greatest discoveries.

In chemistry, Faraday made many discoveries that benefited people. For example, he developed a method of liquefying gases. Today, we use a method much like his original process to manufacture rocket fuel.

Combining chemistry and electricity, the scientist developed a process of *electrolysis*, the decomposition of a chemical compound by the passage of an electrical current through a solution of it, which made it possible to plate metals with other metals or protective coatings. He also contributed to the printing industry by developing electrotype, a metal or composition plate.

Although Faraday touched on many areas, he is best remembered for his *Experimental Researches in Electricity*. He made great strides forward in the fields of electricity and magnetism. Besides discovering the generator, he proved that there was a relation between light and magnetism, and he developed much of the electrical vocabulary that we still use today. For example, electrode, anode, cathode, electrolysis, ion, and lines of force were all terms developed and put to use by Faraday.

Chapter 10

CONCLUSION

Michael Faraday, a boy who grew up in the slums of London, rose to the position of a respected scientist and philosopher. This was not an easy task in nineteenth-century London.

It was Faraday's forceful personality that propelled him to fame; his strong will, his desire to succeed in his research, and his self-pride caused him never to give up on an idea. His stubbornness led him to his great discoveries.

Yet, even more than his research, perhaps Faraday should be remembered for his philosophy. Faraday believed that anyone could become a philosopher and scientist. All that was needed was to get rid of any ideas or thoughts that might influence the thought process. A person's mind must be a blank page, awaiting the arrival of new thoughts and ideas. He was alone among the scientists of his time in believing that the human mind must be free of all prejudices and always willing to accept different, even revolutionary, ideas. This belief led Faraday to seek out other philosophical people and never to lose hope of finding a better world for himself and others through the studies of science and philosophy. Michael Faraday was a proud, kind, humble, and deeply religious person. He felt close to nature and to people and strived all his life to understand them better.

On August 25, 1867, Michael Faraday died at the age of seventy-five, but the discoveries he made in the 1800s have given us limitless opportunities for the future. We are now in the space age and have extended the boundaries of our knowledge beyond planet Earth. Intergalactic space travel will most likely be achieved through the development of a fusion generator, another device that is based on Faraday's discoveries. We should be grateful to Michael Faraday.

GLOSSARY

AETHER. A substance that was imagined to be everywhere. This substance is not matter; it only gives off light.

AMBER. A resinous substance that attracts and repels other objects.

AMPÈRE'S LAW. The magnetic force of an electric current is always around the wire. Faraday proved this to be wrong.

BATTERY. A single electric cell (or group of cells) used as a source of electric current.

BIOLOGIST. A person who studies the life sciences, such as botany or zoology.

CHEMIST. A person who studies the composition of matter and the changes it undergoes.

COMPASS. An instrument for determining direction. It consists of a freely suspended magnetic needle, which, in the Earth's magnetic field, indicates the north and south poles.

CONDUCTOR. Any object that allows for the easy passage of electric current, for example, copper and aluminum.

CONSERVATION OF MATTER. Faraday's theory that forces can be transferred or converted to other forces.

CONTACT ELECTRICITY. Electricity that is produced when objects come in contact with one another.

CURRENT. Electrons moving through a conductor.

ELECTRIFICATION OF MATTER. Refers to being able to put an electrical charge to matter.

ELECTROLYSIS. The passage of electric current through a conducting
   solution (electrolyte)

ELECTROLYTE. A solution that conducts an electric current.

ELECTROMAGNET. A magnet in which the magnetism is produced by
   an electric current.

ELECTROMAGNETIC INDUCTION. Producing an electric current by
   moving a conductor through a magnetic field or by moving a
   magnetic field close to a conductor. Faraday's principle for electric
   motors and generators.

ELECTROMOTIVE FORCE (EMF). Any force that causes an electric
   current to move through a conductor.

ELECTRON. A negatively charged particle of an atom. The only moving
   part of an atom; orbits the nucleus (center).

ENERGY. The ability to do work.

EXPERIMENTAL RESEARCHES IN ELECTRICITY. The three-volume
   work written by Michael Faraday.

FARAD. A term used when measuring the size of electric condensers.

FARADAY. A term used when measuring the amount of electricity with
   a certain chemical effect.

FIELD THEORY. Faraday's ideas on matter as fields of force.

FIRST LAW OF THERMODYNAMICS. Energy cannot be created or
   destroyed but can be transferred or transformed.

FORCE. An influence that creates a push or pull on an object.

FORCE FIELD. The area influenced by magnetic or electromagnetic lines of force.

GALVANOMETER. An instrument used for measuring an electric current.

GENERATOR (Electric). A device that converts mechanical energy into electricity energy.

HENRY. A measure of self-induction.

LAW OF POLES. "Like" poles of a magnet repel; "unlike" poles attract.

MATTER. Anything that has weight and that occupies space.

NEGATIVE CHARGE. Any object that has more electrons than protons has a negative charge.

PHILOSOPHER. A student of or specialist in philosophy.

PHILOSOPHY. The investigation of phenomena (events) of reality; inquiring into the nature of things.

PHYSICIST. A scientist who specializes in physics.

PLAGIARIST. One who steals someone else's ideas or thoughts and then uses them as his or her own.

POLARIZE (Light). To block out vertical light waves in order to limit glare.

POSITIVE CHARGE. Any object that has more protons than electrons has a positive charge.

RADIANT LIGHT. Light rays that make up the red portion of the visible spectrum.

ROYAL INSTITUTION. A society of scientists dedicated to educating the poor by lecturing and doing research.

ROYAL SOCIETY. A prestigious society of scientists dedicated to research, education, and philosophy.

SELF-INDUCTION. When a current moves in the opposite direction of a dying-out current.

THE CITY PHILOSOPHICAL SOCIETY. An organization created by Mr. John Tatum, where young men of poor economic backgrounds could practice philosophy.

Michael Faraday 1791-1867

1791 Michael Faraday is born in Newington, Surrey, England. The first ten amendments to the U.S. Constitution (Bill of Rights) are ratified. Thomas Paine writes *The Rights of Man* (in defense of the French Revolution). Mozart's *Magic Flute* is first performed in Vienna. The waltz becomes fashionable in England. Samuel F.B. Morse, the inventor of the telegraph, is born.

1792 Two political parties are formed in the U.S.: the Republican under Thomas Jefferson, and the Federalist under Alexander Hamilton and John Adams. Shelley, the English poet, is born. Illuminating gas is used in England for the first time.

1793 The Reign of Terror begins in France. Queen Marie Antoinette is executed. The building of the Capitol in Washington, D.C., begins. The Louvre in Paris becomes France's national art gallery. Eli Whitney invents the cotton gin. U.S. law compels escaped slaves to return to their owners.

1794 Mass executions in France. U.S. Navy established. Thomas Paine writes *The Age of Reason*. The song "Auld Lang Syne" by Robert Burns is published. John Trumbull paints his famous painting of *The Declaration of Independence*.

1795 Bread riots and White Terror in Paris. Treaty of San Lorenzo between U.S. and Spain settles boundary with Florida and gives U.S. right to navigate Mississippi. Goya paints his portrait of *The Duchess of Alba*. The first horse-drawn railroad is built in England.

1796 Napoleon marries Josephine de Beauharnais. George Washington, refusing a third term, gives a Farewell Address. John Adams defeats Thomas Jefferson in U.S. presidential election. Edward Jenner, an English physician, introduces a vaccination against smallpox.

1797 Talleyrand becomes French foreign minister. Napoleon defeats Austrians and proclaims Venetian Constitution. Appointed to command forces for the invasion of England, he arrives in Paris. The German astronomer H.W.M. Olbers publishes his method of calculating the orbits of comets. England begins to export iron. John MacArthur introduces Merino sheep to Australia.

1798 French capture Rome and proclaim the Roman Republic. The German inventor Aloys Senefelder invents lithography.

1799 The Royal Institution is founded in London by Count Rumford. Napoleon advances into Syria. Beethoven composes his first symphony. The Rosetta Stone, found near Rosetta, Egypt, makes the deciphering of hieroglyphics possible. The Russian government grants the monopoly of trade in Alaska to the Russian-American Company.

1800 Napoleon establishes himself as first consul, defeats Austrians at Marengo, and conquers Italy. U.S. federal offices are moved from Philadelphia to Washington, D.C., the new capital city. Thomas Jefferson is elected president. The Royal College of Surgeons is founded in London. Alessandro Volta produces electricity from a cell. Sir Humphry Davy publishes a paper on nitrous oxide.

1801 An economic depression hits England. The Faraday family moves to Gilbert Street. Sir Humphry Davy lectures at the Royal Institution and discovers the electric arc. Robert Fulton produces the first submarine, *Nautilus*. The Union Jack becomes the official flag of the United Kingdom of Great Britain and Ireland.

1802 Napoleon becomes the president of the Italian Republic. Beethoven writes his second symphony. John Dalton introduces atomic theory into chemistry. The German naturalist Gottfried Treviranus coins the term "biology." Alexander von Humboldt almost succeeds in climbing Mount Chimborao in Ecuador.

1803 The U.S. buys a large tract of land from the Gulf of Mexico to the northwest, including Louisiana and New Orleans, from France (Louisiana Purchase). Ralph Waldo Emerson is born. Robert Fulton propels a boat by steam power. Henry Shrapnel, an English inventor, invents the artillery shell.

1804 Napoleon is proclaimed emperor. Alexander Hamilton, former U.S. Secretary of the Treasury, is killed in a duel with Aaron Burr. Benjamin Disraeli, the English statesman, is born. The English scientist W.H. Wollaston finds palladium in platinum.

1805 Napoleon is crowned king of Italy in Milan Cathedral. Hans Christian Andersen is born. Beethoven writes the opera *Fidelio*. Rockets are introduced as weapons into the British army.

1806 British occupy the Cape of Good Hope. Napoleon enters Berlin. Sir Humphry Davy discovers the electrolytic method for preparation of potassium and soda.

1807 Robert Fulton's paddle steamer *Clermont* navigates on the Hudson River. The first Ascot Gold Cup horse race is held. England prohibits the slave trade. The first streets are lit by gas in London.

1808 The source of the Ganges River is discovered. Pigtails disappear from men's hair in England. Extensive excavations begin at Pompeii.

1809 James Madison becomes the fourth president of the U.S. Abraham Lincoln is born. Charles Darwin is born. Beethoven composes the Emperor Concerto. Louis Braille, French inventor of a reading system for the blind, is born.

1810 Napoleon annexes several important German cities. Frederic Chopin and Robert Schumann are born. Francois Appert develops techniques for canning food. P.T. Barnum is born.

1811 William Henry Harrison, later president of the U.S., defeats the Indians under Tecumseh at Tippecanoe, Indiana. Amedeo Avogadro, Italian chemist, develops a hypothesis regarding the molecular composition of gases. Johann Meyer, a Swiss mountaineer, climbs the Jungfrau.

1812 The U.S. declares war on Britain. The Brothers Grimm write *Fairy Tales*. The Elgin Marbles are brought to England. The *Comet*, a 25-ton steamship, operates on the Clyde River in Scotland. Sir Humphry Davy writes *Elements of Chemical Philosophy*. Philippe Girard invents a machine for spinning flax.

1813 Prussia and Austria declare war on France. Jane Austen writes *Pride and Prejudice*. Guiseppe Verdi and Richard Wagner are born. The waltz conquers the European ballrooms.

1814 Allied armies defeat the French and enter Paris. Napoleon abdicates and is banished to Elba. The British burn Washington, D.C. The London *Times* is printed by a steam-operated press.

1815 Sir Humphry Davy invents the miner's safety lamp. British road surveyor John McAdam invents roads of crushed stone. The first steam warship is launched—the U.S.S. *Fulton*.

1816 Faraday becomes a lecturer at the Royal Institution. Sir David Brewster invents the kaleidoscope. R.T. Laënnec invents the stethoscope.

1817 James Monroe becomes fifth president of the U.S. Henry David Thoreau is born. U.S. begins construction of the Erie Canal between Buffalo and Albany.

1818 The border between Canada and the U.S. is agreed upon. Karl Marx is born. Professional horse racing begins in the U.S. The *Savannah* becomes the first steamship to cross the Atlantic (26 days).

1819 The future Queen Victoria is born. Walt Whitman is born. Danish physicist Hans C. Oersted discovers electromagnetism. David Napier constructs the flatbed cylinder press for printing.

1820 Faraday pursues the study of electricity. André Ampère writes *Laws of the Electrodynamic Action*. The Missouri Compromise: Maine enters the Union as a free state and Missouri as a slave state. The Venus de Milo is discovered. "Ballown," a kind of soccer, is played for the first time in the U.S. Florence Nightingale is born.

1821 Michael Faraday is nominated to become a fellow of the famed Royal Society. Faraday discovers the fundamentals of electromagnetic rotation. James Monroe begins his second term as president of the U.S. Peru proclaims its independence from Spain, followed by Guatemala, Panama, and Santo Domingo. Napoleon dies. Champollion deciphers Egyptian hieroglyphics, using the Rosetta Stone. Sir Charles Wheatstone demonstrated sound reproduction.

1822 Daguerre and Bouton invent the diorama, paintings illuminated in a dark room to give the illusion of reality. A.J. Fresnel perfects lenses for lighthouses. Gregor Mendel, founder of the science of genetics, is born. The streets of Boston are lit by gas. The world's first iron railroad bridge is built in England.

1823 Mexico becomes a republic. The Monroe Doctrine closes the American continent to colonial settlements by European powers. Faraday succeeds in liquefying chlorine. Charles Macintosh invents a waterproof fabric. Charles Babbage attempts to make a calculating machine. The Royal Thames Yacht Club is founded. Rugby Football originates at Rugby School, England.

1824 The U.S. House of Representatives elects John Quincy Adams president when none of the four candidates wins a majority. The National Gallery in London is founded. The Erie Canal is finished.

1825 Faraday becomes director of the laboratory at the Royal Institution. Faraday succeeds in isolating benzene. William Sturgeon produces the first electromagnet. John Quincy Adams is inaugurated as sixth president of the U.S. The Stockton-Darlington railroad line opens in England—the first line to carry passengers. A Baseball Club is organized in Rochester, New York. Horse-drawn buses begin operating in London.

1826 James Fenimore Cooper writes *The Last of the Mohicans*. Mendelssohn writes the overture to *A Midsummer Night's Dream*. André Ampère writes his work on *Electrodynamics*. The first railroad tunnel is built in England. The Unter den Linden in Berlin is lit by gas.

1827 Beethoven dies. J.J. Audubon publishes his *Birds of North America*. Joseph Niepce produces photographs on a metal plate. George S. Ohm formulates Ohm's Law, defining electrical current potential and resistance. James Simpson constructs a sand filter for the purification of London's water supply. Karl Baedeker begins publishing his travel guides. Sulfur friction matches are introduced by John Walker.

1828 Andrew Jackson defeats John Quincy Adams in the U.S. presidential election. Alexandre Dumas père writes *The Three Musketeers*. Noah Webster publishes the *American Dictionary of the English Language*. Construction begins on the Baltimore & Ohio Railroad, the first railroad built in the U.S. for the transportation of passengers and freight.

1829 L.J.M. Daguerre forms a partnership with J.N. Niepce for the development of their photographic invention. Sir Humphry Davy, the English chemist and friend of Faraday's, dies. American physicist John Henry constructs an early version of the electromagnetic motor. James Smithson, British chemist, bequeaths 100,000 pounds to found the Smithsonian Institution in Washington, D.C. Buses become part of London transport. The first Oxford-Cambridge boat race takes place at Henley. The first U.S. patent on a typewriter is granted to William B. Burt of Detroit. The London Zoo is founded.

1830 In a debate with Robert Y. Hayne, Daniel Webster negates the States' Rights Doctrine. The American poet Emily Dickinson is born. The Royal Geographic Society is founded in London. Stiff collars become part of men's dress. Ladies' skirts grow shorter; sleeves become enormous; hats extremely large, ornamented with flowers and ribbons.

1831 Belgium separates from the Netherlands. Negro Nat Turner leads the Virginia slave revolt. Chloroform is simultaneously invented by Samuel Guthrie (Amer.) and Justus von Liebig (Ger.). Charles Darwin sails as a naturalist on a surveying expedition to South America, New Zealand, and Australia on the H.M.S. *Beagle*. Faraday carries out a series of experiments demonstrating the discovery of electromagnetic induction. William Lloyd Garrison begins publishing the abolitionist periodical *The Liberator* in Boston. London Bridge is opened. The first horse-drawn buses appear in New York. George M. Pullman, designer of railroad cars, is born.

1832 Andrew Jackson is reelected president of the U.S. under the banner of the newly styled "Democratic party." The word "socialism" comes into use in English and French. Louisa May Alcott is born. Horatio Alger is born. Lewis Carroll is born. Faraday proposes pectorial representation of electric and magnetic lines of force. The first French railroad line begins to carry passengers. The manufacture of friction matches is well established in Europe. Charles Carroll, the last surviving signer of the Declaration of Independence, dies. The first horse-drawn trolleys operate in New York.

1833 Davy Crockett's autobiography becomes a best seller. The great von Schlegel translation of Shakespeare into German is completed. Johannes Brahms is born. K.F. Gauss and Wilhelm E. Weber devise the electromagnetic telegraph which functions over a distance of 9,000 feet. Alfred Nobel, Swedish chemist and engineer, and donor of the Nobel Prize fund, is born. Slavery is abolished in the British Empire. Sir John Ross returns from his second Arctic expedition in which he discovered the magnetic North Pole.

1834 Abraham Lincoln (at 25) enters politics as an assemblyman in the Illinois Legislature. Victor Hugo writes *The Hunchback of Notre Dame*. F.A. Bartholdi, sculptor of the Statue of Liberty, is born. Faraday writes *The Law of Electrolysis*. Cyrus Hall McCormick patents his reaping machine. Two-wheeled, one-horse Hansom cabs are introduced in London. Walter Hunt of New York constructs one of the first sewing machines.

1835 Texas declares its right to secede from Mexico. Hans Christian Andersen publishes the first four of his 168 tales for children. Mark Twain is born. Halley's comet reappears. The first efforts to propel railroad vehicles by electric batteries are made. U.S. showman Phineas T. Barnum begins his career with the exhibition of a black woman alleged to be George Washington's nurse and over 160 years old. Samuel Colt takes out an English patent for his single-barreled pistol and rifle. Charles Chubb patents a burglar-proof safe. The first German railroad line opens between Nuremberg and Furth.

1836 Faraday perfects his experiment on induced current, the foundation of electromagnetic theory. Davy Crockett is killed at the Alamo. Dickens's *The Pickwick Papers* is serialized. Ampère, the French physicist, dies. Asa Gray writes the first textbook in botany. The first cricket match is played in London. Betsy Ross dies.

1837 Martin Van Buren is inaugurated as eighth president of the U.S. Victoria becomes queen of Great Britain. Benjamin Disraeli delivers his first speech to the House of Commons. *Twice-told Tales*, by Nathaniel Hawthorne, becomes a best seller. Horace Mann begins educational reforms in Massachusetts. Wheatstone and W.F. Cooke patent the electric telegraph. Samuel Morse exhibits his electric telegraph at the College of the City of New York. The first boat race in the U.S. is held at Poughkeepsie, New York. The first Canadian railroad opens. England introduces official birth registration. E.P. Lovejoy, editor of an abolitionist newspaper, is murdered by a mob in Alton, Illinois. America suffers a financial and economic panic.

1838 Queen Victoria is crowned. *Oliver Twist* and *Nicholas Nickleby* by Charles Dickens become best sellers. The National Gallery in London opens. The 703-ton steamer *Sirius* sails with 100 passengers from London to New York.

1839 The First Opium War breaks out between Britain and China. Poe writes *The Fall of the House of Usher*. American traveler John Lloyd Stephens discovers and examines the antiquities of the ancient Maya culture in Central America. Two British ships, the *Erebus* and the *Terror*, set out on an Antarctic voyage. Charles Goodyear makes possible the commercial use of rubber by his discovery of the process of vulcanization. Moritz Jacobi of St. Petersburg, Russia, announces his process of electrotyping and makes duplicate plates for relief printing. Carl August Steinheil, a Swiss physicist, builds the first electric clock. The first baseball game is played in Cooperstown, New York. The first bicycle is constructed by Scottish inventor Kirkpatrick Macmillan. John D. Rockefeller is born. Samuel Cunard starts a transatlantic shipping line. W.H. Fox Talbot claims that he had success with photographic experiments before Daguerre and communicates his results to the Royal Society.

1840 Queen Victoria marries Prince Albert. James Fenimore Cooper's *The Pathfinder* becomes a best seller. A statue of Lord Nelson is erected in Trafalgar Square in London. Construction begins on the Houses of Parliament. Swiss naturalist Louis Agassiz publishes his work on the movements and effects of glaciers. Liebig discovers the fundamentals of artificial fertilizer. Criminals are transported from England to New South Wales.

1841 Britain's sovereignty is proclaimed over Hong Kong. William Henry Harrison, ninth president of the U.S., dies one month after his inauguration. James Fenimore Cooper writes *The Deerslayer*. Dickens's novel *The Old Curiosity Shop* becomes a best seller. Scottish surgeon James Braid discovers hypnosis. English mechanical engineer Sir Joseph Whitworth proposes standard screw threads. Barnum opens the American Museum, an exhibition of freaks, curios, etc., in New York City. The first university degrees are granted to women in America.

1842 The Webster-Ashburton treaty defines the border between Canada and the U.S. The Treaty of Nanking ends the Opium War between Britain and China and confirms the cession of Hong Kong to Britain. The Orange Free State is set up by the Boers. Joseph Henry discovers the oscillatory character of electrical discharge. American physician Crawford W. Long uses ether to produce surgical anesthesia. American naval officer Matthew F. Maury begins his researches in oceanography. The polka, a lively dance of Czech origin, comes into fashion. Queen Victoria makes her first railroad journey.

1843 The British Archaeological Association and the Royal Archaeological Institute of Great Britain and Ireland are founded. John C. Fremont crosses the Rocky Mountains to California. Congress grants S.F.B. Morse $30,000 to build the first telegraph line (Washington to Baltimore). Skiing begins as a sport.

1844 James Knox Polk is elected eleventh president of the U.S. *The Count of Monte Cristo* becomes a best seller. Wood-pulp paper is invented by Friedrich Gottlob Keller. French missionaries Evariste R. Huc and Joseph Gabet begin journey from China to Tibet.

1845 The Maori stage an uprising against British rule in New Zealand. The first submarine cable is laid across the English Channel. Joshua Heilman patents a machine for combing cotton and wool. The U.S. Naval Academy is opened at Annapolis. The Knickerbocker Baseball Club codifies the rules of baseball.

1846 Brigham Young leads the Mormons to the Great Salt Lake in Utah. The Opèra in Paris is lit by electric arc lighting. John Deere constructs a steel plow. The sewing machine is patented by Elias Howe. The German botanist H. von Mohl identifies protoplasm. The optical factory of Carl Zeiss is founded in Jena. The first painted Christmas card is designed in England.

1847 Charlotte Brontë publishes *Jane Eyre*. Emily Brontë publishes *Wuthering Heights*. Thomas Alva Edison is born. Evaporated milk is made for the first time. The first Swiss railroad opens between Baden and Zurich. Alexander Graham Bell is born. Gold discoveries in California lead to the first gold rush. The Hamburg-America steamship line is founded.

1848 Revolutions break out in Paris, Venice, Berlin, and Milan. Switzerland becomes a federal union. Spiritualism becomes popular in the U.S. The first appendectomy is performed. The first settlers arrive in New Zealand.

1849 Zachary Taylor is inaugurated as president of the U.S. *Who's Who* begins publication. The French physicist Armand Fizeau measures the speed of light. Amelia Bloomer begins American women's dress reform.

1850 Henry Clay's compromise slavery resolutions are laid before the U.S. Senate. Elizabeth Barrett Browning writes *Sonnets from the Portuguese*. Hawthorne writes *The Scarlet Letter*. Jenny Lind tours the U.S. under the management of P.T. Barnum. R.W. Bunsen produces the gas burner. Hermann von Helmholtz establishes the speed of the nervous impulse. Stephenson's cast-iron railroad bridge is opened at Newcastle, England.

1851 Hawthorne writes *The House of Seven Gables*. Melville writes *Moby Dick*. Verdi composes *Rigoletto*. Isaac Singer devises the continuous-stitch sewing machine. Franz Neumann develops the law of electromagnetic induction. the schooner *America* wins a race around the Isle of Wight and brings the America's Cup to the U.S. The first double-decker bus is introduced. Gold is found in Victoria, New South Wales, Australia. The *New York Times* begins publication.

1852 Franklin Pierce is elected the fourteenth president of the U.S. Harriet Beecher Stowe writes *Uncle Tom's Cabin*. Herbert Spencer first uses the word "evolution." The Niagara Falls suspension bridge is built. A saltwater aquarium is opened in London.

1853 Georges Haussmann begins reconstruction of the Paris boulevards. Vincent van Gogh is born. Wagner completes his tetralogy *The Ring of the Nibelungen*. The first railroad is built through the Alps, from Vienna to Trieste. Vaccination against smallpox is made compulsory in England. The largest tree in the world, the Wellington gigantea, is discovered in California.

1854 Commodore M.C. Perry negotiates the first U.S. treaty with Japan. The Republican party is formed. Thoreau writes *Walden*. George Eastman, American photographic pioneer, is born. German watchmaker Heinrich Goebel invents the first form of the electric light bulb.

1855 Longfellow writes *The Song of Hiawatha*. Walt Whitman writes *Leaves of Grass*. Livingstone discovers Victoria Falls in Africa. Paris holds a Worlds Fair. Florence Nightingale introduces hygienic standards into military hospitals during the Crimean War. The first iron Cunard steamer crosses the Atlantic in nine and a half days. Ferdinand de Lesseps is granted concession by France to build the Suez Canal.

1856 Flaubert writes *Madame Bovary*. Sir Henry Bessemer introduces the converter in his process for making steel. Sigmund Freud is born. The first Australian cricket match is held. Big Ben at the British Houses of Parliament is cast at a Whitechapel foundry.

1857 James Buchanan is inaugurated as the fifteenth president of the U.S. The Indians stage a mutiny against British rule. The National Portrait Gallery is opened in London. Robert Baden-Powell, founder of the Boy Scout movement, is born. E.G. Otis installs the first safety elevator. A transatlantic cable is laid. Czar Alexander II begins the emancipation of the serfs in Russia.

1858 Joseph Lister studies coagulation of the blood. The Suez Canal Company is formed. In England, South Foreland lighthouse is lit by electricity. The S.S. *Great Eastern*, the largest ship of her time, is launched. The National Association of Baseball Players is organized in America. The first transatlantic cable is completed by Cyrus W. Field. The Lincoln-Douglas debates are held in Illinois.

1859 Abolitionist John Brown is seized at Harpers Ferry, Virginia. The first commercially productive oil well is drilled near Titusville, Pennsylvania.Dickens writes *A Tale of Two Cities*. Tennyson writes *Idylls of the King*. Darwin writes *On the Origin of Species*. R.L.G. Plante invents the first practical storage battery. The steamroller is invented. A Frenchman, Charles Blondi, crosses Niagara Falls on a tightrope. Work on the Suez Canal is begun under the direction of Ferdinand de Lesseps.

1860 Abraham Lincoln is elected president of the U.S. The first pony-express line is started between Sacramento, California and St. Joseph, Missouri. Lenoir constructs the first practical internal combustion engine. Baseball becomes popular in New York and Boston. Skiing begins as a competitive sport. The first horse-drawn tram begins operation.

1861 Seven southern states set up the Confederate States of America with Jefferson Davis as president. Confederate forces repel Union forces at the Battle of Bull Run. The first transcontinental telegraph begins operation in the U.S. Dickens writes *Great Expectations*. Daily weather forecasts are begun in Britain.

1862 Lion Foucault successfully measures the speed of light. Johann von Lamont discovers earth currents. Julius Sachs, a German botanist, demonstrates that starch is produced by photosynthesis. The English cricket team tours Australia for the first time. Swiss humanist Jean Henri Dunant proposes the foundation of an international relief organization—the Red Cross.

1863 Lincoln issues the Emancipation Proclamation, freeing "all slaves in areas still in rebellion." Lincoln reads his Gettysburg Address, at the dedication of a military cemetery. Henry Ford is born. Construction of an underground railroad is begun in London. U.S. Congress establishes free mail delivery. Roller skating is introduced to America. French photographer A.F. Nader makes an ascent in his balloon "Le Géant."

1864 General Sherman marches through Georgia. Ulysses S. Grant becomes commander-in-chief of the Union armies. Abraham Lincoln is reelected president. Tolstoi writes *War and Peace*. Louis Pasteur invents pasteurization (for wine). The first salmon cannery in the U.S. opens in Washington, California. "In God We Trust" first appears on U.S. coins.

1865 Lee surrenders at Appomattox. Lincoln is shot at Ford's Theater. He is succeeded by Andrew Johnson. The Civil War Ends. Lewis Carroll writes *Alice's Adventures in Wonderland*. Joseph Lister initiates antiseptic surgery. Gregor Mendel enunciates his Law of Heredity. The first carpet sweeper comes into use. The London Metropolitan Fire Service is established. The first sleeping cars, designed by Pullman, appear in the U.S.

1866 The Fourteenth Amendment to the U.S. Constitution prohibits voting discrimination, denies government office to certain Civil War rebels, and repudiates Confederate war debts. Dostoyevsky writes *Crime and Punishment*. Degas begins to paint ballet scenes. The Aeronautical Society of Great Britain is founded. Alfred Nobel invents dynamite. English engineer Robert Whitehead invents the underwater torpedo.

1867 Alaska is sold by Russia to the U.S. for $7.2 million. The British North America Act establishes the Dominion of Canada. The Paris World's Fair introduces Japanese art to the West. Gold is discovered in Wyoming. Livingstone explores the Congo. Pierre Michaux begins to manufacture bicycles. A railroad is completed through the Brenner Pass. Diamonds are discovered in South Africa. Michael Faraday dies.

INDEX- *Page numbers in boldface type indicate illustrations.*

ABOUT THE AUTHOR

Martin J. Gutnik is the author of twenty children and young adult books. He is an elementary science specialist in the Shorewood, Wisconsin public schools, as well as a noted ecologist. Using a unique Wisconsin environmental system, which he created and built, he teaches all ages about the interrelationships of plant and animal life. He is also a frequent lecturer on body dependency substances and sex education. Mr. Gutnik lives with his wife, Natalie, and their family in Bayside, Wisconsin.